02/07
RB $24.95

Why Is This Day Special?

A New Baby

Jillian Powell

A⁺
Smart Apple Media

First published in 2005 by Franklin Watts
96 Leonard Street, London EC2A 4XD

Franklin Watts Australia
45–51 Huntley Street, Alexandria, NSW 2015

Series editor: Sarah Peutrill, Art director: Jonathan Hair, Designer: Ian Thompson, Picture researcher: Diana Morris, Reading consultant: Margaret Perkins, Institute of Education, University of Reading

Picture credits: Kevin Cozad/O'Brien Productions/Corbis: 24. Francisco Cruz/Superstock: 7t. DPA/TSS/Image Works/Topham: front cover main, 10. Chris Fairclough/Franklin Watts: 11, 12t, 13t, 15b, 15m, 17b. Craig Hammell/Corbis: 25t. Robert van der Hilst/Corbis: 22. Dennis Macdonald/Alamy: 27b. Ray Moller/Franklin Watts: front cover bottom, 7b, 12b, 15t, 17t, 20, 21b, 27t, 27m. Bazuki Muhammed/Reuters/Corbis: 16, 23. John Nordell/Topham: 14. Rikke Steenvinkel-Nordenhof/Polfoto/Topham: 8. Michel Renaudeau/Hoa-qui: 9t. Helene Rogers/Art Director/Trip: 13b, 21t, 25b. Gregor Schmid/Corbis: 19. Superstock: 9b.

With thanks to Lisa and Richard Gooch for permission to use their photographs.

Published in the United States by Smart Apple Media
2140 Howard Drive West, North Mankato, Minnesota 56003

Library of Congress Cataloging-in-Publication Data

Powell, Jillian.
A new baby / by Jillian Powell.
p. cm. — (Why is this day special?)
Includes index.
ISBN-13 : 978-1-58340-949-7
1. Birth customs—Juvenile literature. I. Title.

GT2460.P69 2006
392.1'2—dc22   2005052058

9 8 7 6 5 4 3 2 1

Contents

A new arrival

The birth of a baby is a happy and exciting time.

All around the world, people celebrate a new baby. Some ways of celebrating are hundreds of years old.

People welcome the baby into a family, a community, and sometimes a religion.

A baby is starting out on a new life. There is a lot to look forward to, such as the baby's first smile, first words, and first steps.

It's a special moment when a mother holds her newborn baby for the first time.

At a baby shower, friends and family bring gifts for the mother and her baby.

In some countries, a special party is held before a baby is born. This is a called a baby shower. Friends give gifts to the mother-to-be, and there are decorations, games to play, and a special cake to eat.

" My aunt held a baby shower and we played lots of games. We all had to make a baby from playdough, and my aunt gave a prize for the best baby! "

Lisa, age 8

Greetings

When a baby is born, everyone wants to say hello!

Family and friends usually visit the mother and baby as soon as they can.

> " I remember going to the hospital to see my sister Kareena when she was born. I was scared to hold her at first, she looked so tiny. "
>
> *Satish, age 8*

Brothers, sisters, grandparents, uncles, and aunts all want to see the new baby and welcome him or her to their family.

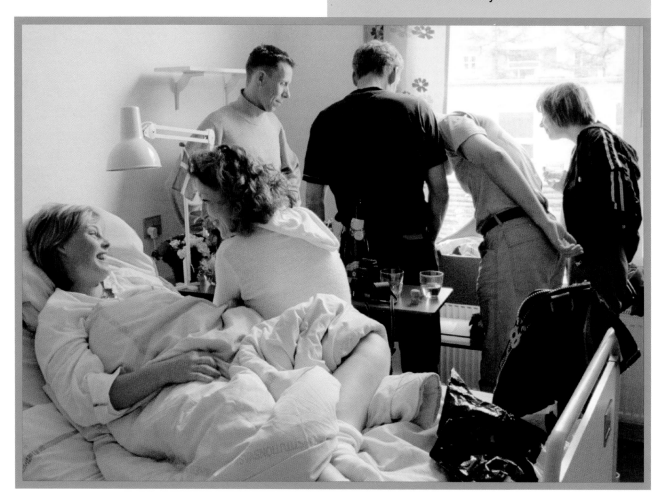

A baby is welcomed with music by his father and community in Equatorial Guinea, Africa.

In some African villages, people sing songs and play music to welcome a baby.

Everywhere, cradlesongs, or lullabies, are sung to welcome a new baby. This helps the baby to sleep and feel loved.

A great-grandmother cares for the new arrival in her family.

Naming a baby

Soon after a baby is born, he or she is given a name, usually by the baby's parents.

In some religions, a naming ceremony is held.

Hindu babies are named in a special ceremony 12 days after they are born.

> **"** *My name is Sita, after the wife of the Hindu god Lord Rama. A priest read my horoscope after I was born and suggested the name to my mom and dad.* **"**
>
> Sita, age 7

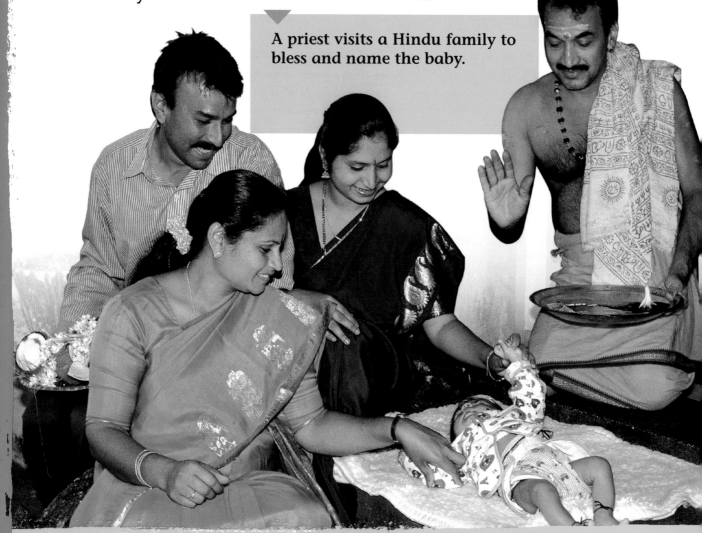

A priest visits a Hindu family to bless and name the baby.

Sikh babies have their naming ceremony in a *gurdwara*.

The parents sit in front of the Sikh holy book.

> The Sikh holy book is called the Guru Granth Sahib.

A reader opens the book and reads the first word on the left-hand page. The parents choose a name that begins with the same letter as that word.

Some African families write different names on pieces of paper. They choose the name from the first piece of paper that the baby touches.

Tutu

Rafiki

Abayoni

Kenyi

11

Prayer and religion

Some babies are also welcomed into their family's religion. Some of the first words a baby hears may be a special prayer.

Babies are welcomed into the Christian religion with prayers at their baptism or christening.

This is an Anglican christening. The candles stand for the light of Jesus Christ, who will guide the baby through his life.

66 *When I was christened, I wore a christening dress. Mom says if I have babies, they can wear it too.* 99
Judith, age 8

Christian parents choose godparents. These are friends or relatives who promise to help bring up the child as a Christian.

Baby boys are circumcised to welcome them into the Jewish religion. The ceremony ends with a prayer.

Girls may also be welcomed with a ceremony of prayer and blessing.

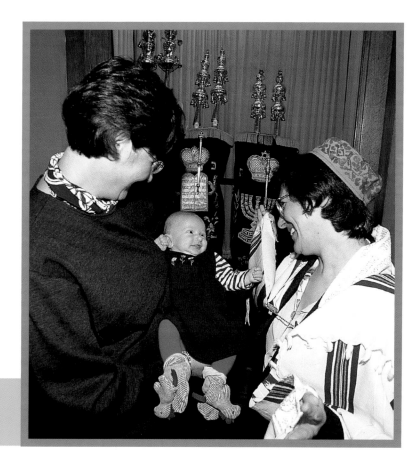

This Jewish girl has been blessed by a rabbi.

Buddhist families sometimes ask a monk to chant from Buddhist writings and bless the baby.

This Buddhist monk is blessing a baby girl.

A clean start

A baby is starting a new life, and some religions have ceremonies to celebrate this.

In Japan, babies are taken to a Shinto shrine a month after they are born.

The priest says prayers and waves a *tamagushi* of bamboo and paper over the baby's head. This is to give the baby a clean start in life.

This Shinto priest is waving a *tamagushi*. The paper strips are white, which is the color of purity in the Shinto religion.

Some African families break open a coconut and sprinkle a baby with the milk. They ask God to pour blessings on the baby.

The hair on a Hindu boy's head is shaved off when he is one year old.

At a Christian baptism, the priest pours a little holy water over the baby's head.

Hindus believe that shaving hair takes away badness from past lives.

A Christian baptism ceremony. The curate pours holy water from a font.

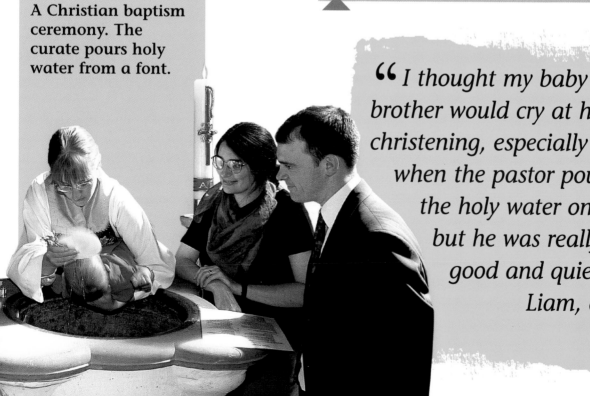

66 I thought my baby brother would cry at his christening, especially when the pastor poured the holy water on him, but he was really good and quiet. 99
Liam, age 9

Sweet foods

Some religions have a custom of giving newborn babies sweet foods to bring them sweetness and good luck in life.

Muslims put a drop of sugar, honey, or date juice onto a baby's tongue.

A Malaysian Muslim baby boy is given a taste of sugar.

66 *We had a little ceremony for my brother when he and Mom came home from the hospital. We put a bit of sugar on his tongue and said a prayer to welcome him as a Muslim.* 99

Amina, age 9

Hindus write the holy word *Aum* on the baby's tongue in honey, using a golden pen. This word is used in Hindu prayer and blessings. It stands for the names of the three most important Hindu gods.

Putting honey on a baby's tongue gives him or her a first taste of sweet food.

Sikhs give a little *amrit*, or sweet water, to a baby after his naming ceremony. It welcomes the baby into the Sikh community.

The family and friends of a Sikh baby eat a sweet pudding called *kara prashad.*

Kara prashad is made from flour, butter, and sugar.

Announcements

There are many ways of announcing, or telling people about, a birth.

Everyone will be waiting to hear about a new baby, so the news is passed around as soon as the baby is born.

Mom and Dad kept the newspaper with my birth announcement in. It's quite interesting reading what was in the news when I was born!

Jamila, age 8

Lisa and Richard Gooch are pleased to announce the birth of their baby girl.

Lauren Grace was born on March 16th at 4:35 P.M. She weighed 6 pounds and 3 ounces (2.8 kg).

Some people put a notice in a newspaper or on a Web site announcing their baby's birth.

The parents often save their announcement.

Parents often send out letters to tell their family and friends they have a new baby.

Some families put signs up outside their house to announce their child's birth.

A pole announces a birth in Bavaria, Germany. The details of the baby's birth are written on a paper heart at the bottom. The stork on the top is a traditional symbol of a new baby.

Greek families have a special way to announce a baptism. They send a photo of the invitation with the baby next to it.

Sending a photo is a traditional way to invite guests to a Greek baptism.

Cards and gifts

Many people give cards and gifts to a newborn baby.

Sometimes people give soft toys to put in a stroller or cradle.

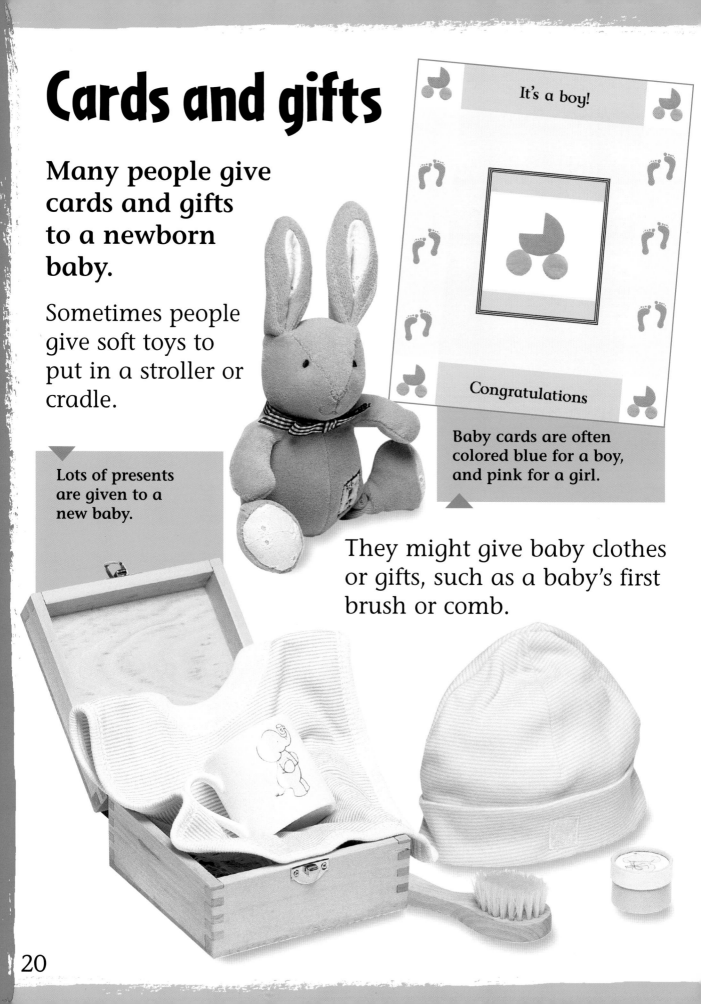

It's a boy!

Congratulations

Baby cards are often colored blue for a boy, and pink for a girl.

Lots of presents are given to a new baby.

They might give baby clothes or gifts, such as a baby's first brush or comb.

In some countries, traditional gifts for luck are given.

Coins may be given to bring wealth. Salt is given for health, cotton for a long life, and sugar or chocolates are given for sweetness.

> Hindu families sometimes give chocolates in a pretty box for good luck.

Silver spoons, crosses, rattles, and other silver gifts are often given for a christening. Silver is believed to be lucky.

When I was born, my aunt gave me a christening spoon. I have to keep it really carefully because it's as old as me!

Jacqui, age 9

21

Celebrations

In many countries, people have a party to celebrate the arrival of a new baby.

They get together for a drink to "wet the baby's head."

A party in Peru to celebrate the arrival of a baby.

In Peru, they celebrate a new baby by drinking *chicha*, a beer made from corn. They celebrate again when a baby boy gets his first haircut or a girl has her ears pierced.

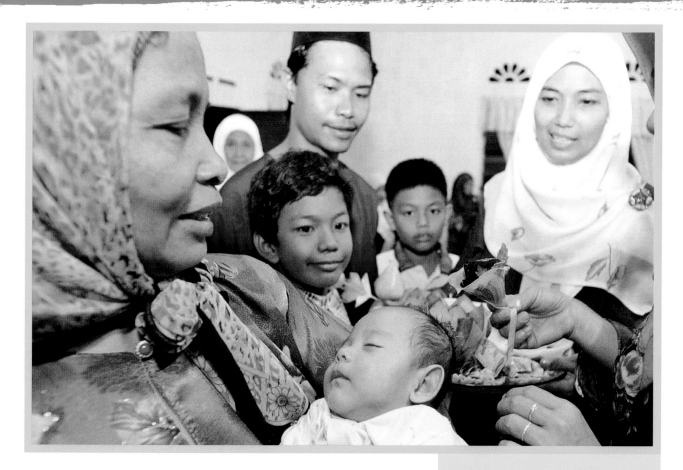

A Muslim boy is blessed with holy water at the feast after his naming ceremony.

Food is also important at birth celebrations.

In Muslim birth ceremonies, the baby's family invites all the villagers to a feast seven days after the birth.

" We had a party after my sister was christened. All the family came, and we had a christening cake. "

Melissa, age 8

After a Christian christening, people sometimes eat a special cake, usually made from fruit. Sometimes the cake is the top layer of the couple's wedding cake, which they have saved.

Marking the birth

One way of marking, or remembering, a birth is to plant a tree. The tree will grow as the child grows.

Birth trees are planted in many parts of the world. In Switzerland, apple trees are planted for the birth of a boy, and nut trees for a girl.

> 66 *When I was born, Dad planted a rose in our garden. It's called 'Congratulations,' but I call it my rose!* 99
>
> Bethan, age 7

In different countries, an ash may be planted for a long life, a fig tree for wisdom, an olive for peace, or a maple for luck.

An apple tree in Switzerland that was planted for the birth of a boy. Apple trees bear fruit after about 15 years.

In Jewish families, it is traditional to plant a cedar tree for a boy and a pine tree for a girl.

When the child is old enough to marry, his or her birth tree may be cut down to make a *huppah*. This is a cover on four poles under which he or she will marry.

Another way to mark the birth is to make a print or mold of the baby's hand.

A pine tree being planted for a Jewish baby girl.

These babies' hands have been printed into a mold and saved with a photograph.

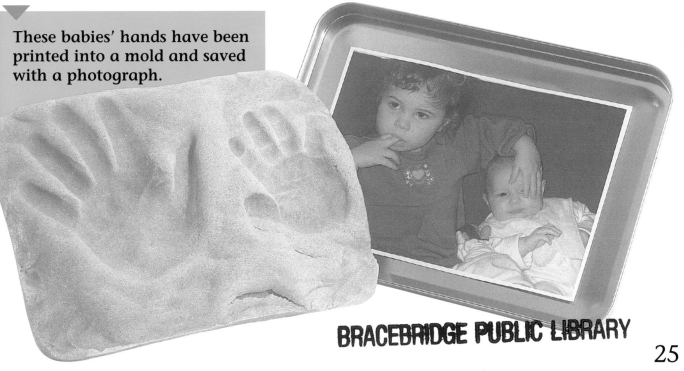

Birth memories

The birth of a baby is a special time for families and friends to enjoy. Many people want to keep things to remind them of their special time.

The parents take photos of the baby and keep them in a family album, or make a baby book.

In a baby book, the parents write down everything about the early days of their baby, so their child can read it when he or she is older.

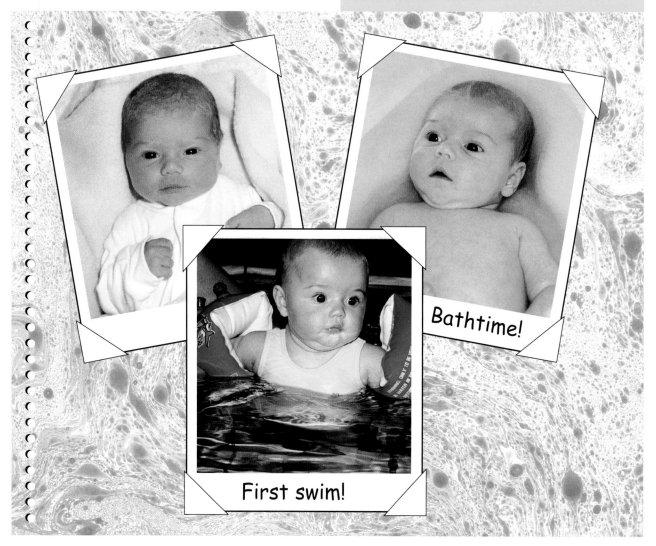

Bathtime!

First swim!

Some families keep the baby's name tag from the hospital where he or she was born, or the baby's first tiny shoes.

If a baby is born in a hospital, he or she is given a name tag, which the baby wears on his or her wrist.

66 *My mom kept my first coat that my grandma knitted for me. I can't believe it's mine, because it looks so small!* 99

Alex, age 8

The day a baby is born is celebrated every year as his or her birthday.

First birthdays are often important days. In some religions, the first birthday is marked by giving special gifts. Some families have a party for their one-year-old.

One candle on the cake marks a first birthday.

Glossary

aum sometimes *om*—a holy symbol and sound in the Hindu religion.

baptism a ceremony in which a baby is welcomed into the Christian religion.

circumcision when a small piece of skin is cut from a baby boy's penis.

curate an assistant to a pastor in a Christian church.

font a basin in a church that holds water for a baptism.

godparent a person chosen by a baby's parents who promises to give the child love, and to support as a Christian as he or she grows up.

gurdwara a Sikh temple.

Guru Granth Sahib the Sikh holy book.

holy water water that has been blessed.

huppah An open cover under which a Jewish bride and groom are married.

kara prashad a sweet pudding shared at Sikh ceremonies.

lullabies songs to help a baby go to sleep.

prayer words said when a person talks to God.

priest a person who leads religious ceremonies.

rabbi a person who leads Jewish ceremonies.

shrine a place that a religious group believes is holy.

tamagushi a branch tied with paper strips used in a Shinto ceremony.

Religions in this book

Buddhism
Follower: Buddhist
Important figure: Siddhartha Gautama, the Buddha
Gods: None—the Buddha did not want people to worship him as a God
Places of worship: Viharas (temples or monasteries), stupas (shrines)
Holy books: Tirpitaka (Pali Canon), Diamond Sutra, and others

Christianity
Follower: Christian
Important figure: Jesus Christ, Son of God
God: One God as Father, Son, and Holy Spirit
Places of worship: Churches, cathedrals, and chapels
Holy book: The Bible

Hinduism
Follower: Hindu
Gods and goddesses: Many, including Brahma (the Creator), Vishnu (the Protector), and Shiva (the Destroyer)
Places of worship: Mandirs (temples) and shrines
Holy books: Vedas, Upanishads, Ramayana, Mahabharata

Islam
Follower: Muslim
Important figure: The Prophet Muhammad
God: Allah
Place of worship: Mosque
Holy book: The Koran

Judaism
Follower: Jew
Important figures: Abraham, Isaac, Jacob, and Moses
Gods: One God, the creator
Place of worship: Synagogues
Holy books: Tenakh, Torah, Talmud

Shinto
Follower: Shinto
Important figures: Ancestors, nature spirits, dead heroes
God: Kami
Places of worship: Shrines
Holy books: Kojiki, Nihon shoki

Sikhism
Follower: Sikh
Important figure: Guru Nanak
Gods: One God
Place of worship: Gurdwaras (temples)
Holy book: Guru Granth Sahib

Index